RUNAW

# RUNAWAYS

WRITER: **BRIAN K. VAUGHAN**
PENCILS: **ADRIAN ALPHONA**
INKS: **DAVID NEWBOLD** (#1-5) & **CRAIG YEUNG** (#6)
COLORS: **BRIAN REBER**
LETTERS: **PAUL TUTRONE** (#1), **CHRIS ELIOPOULOS** (#2-4)
& **RANDY GENTILE** (#5-6)
COVER ART: **JO CHEN**
COLLECTION COVER: **TAKESHI MIYAZAWA** & **BRIAN REBER**
ASSISTANT EDITORS: **STEPHANIE MOORE** & **MACKENZIE CADENHEAD**
EDITOR: **C.B. CEBULSKI**

***RUNAWAYS*** CREATED BY **BRIAN K. VAUGHAN** & **ADRIAN ALPHONA**

COLLECTION EDITOR: JENNIFER GRÜNWALD
ASSOCIATE MANAGING EDITOR: KATERI WOODY
ASSOCIATE EDITOR: SARAH BRUNSTAD
EDITOR, SPECIAL PROJECTS: MARK D. BEAZLEY
VP PRODUCTION & SPECIAL PROJECTS: JEFF YOUNGQUIST
SVP PRINT, SALES & MARKETING: DAVID GABRIEL

EDITOR IN CHIEF: AXEL ALONSO
CHIEF CREATIVE OFFICER: JOE QUESADA
PUBLISHER: DAN BUCKLEY
EXECUTIVE PRODUCER: ALAN FINE

**RUNAWAYS VOL. 1: PRIDE & JOY.** Contains material originally published in magazine form as RUNAWAYS #1-6. Second edition. First printing 2016. ISBN# 978-1-302-90499-9. Published by MARVEL WORLDWIDE, INC., a subsidiary of MARVEL ENTERTAINMENT, LLC. OFFICE OF PUBLICATION: 135 West 50th Street, New York, NY 10020.  **Printed in the U.S.A.** ALAN FINE, President, Marvel Entertainment; DAN BUCKLEY, President, TV, Publishing & Brand Management; JOE QUESADA, Chief Creative Officer; TOM BREVOORT, SVP of Publishing; DAVID BOGART, SVP of Business Affairs & Operations, Publishing & Partnership; C.B. CEBULSKI, VP of Brand Management & Development, Asia; DAVID GABRIEL, SVP of Sales & Marketing, Publishing; JEFF YOUNGQUIST, VP of Production & Special Projects; DAN CARR, Executive Director of Publishing Technology; ALEX MORALES, Director of Publishing Operations; SUSAN CRESPI, Production Manager; STAN LEE, Chairman Emeritus. For information regarding advertising in Marvel Comics or on Marvel.com, please contact Vit DeBellis, Integrated Sales Manager, at vdebellis@marvel.com. For Marvel subscription inquiries, please call 888-511-5480. **Manufactured between 9/16/2016 and 10/24/2016 by LSC COMMUNICATIONS INC., SALEM, VA, USA.**

10 9 8 7 6 5 4 3 2 1

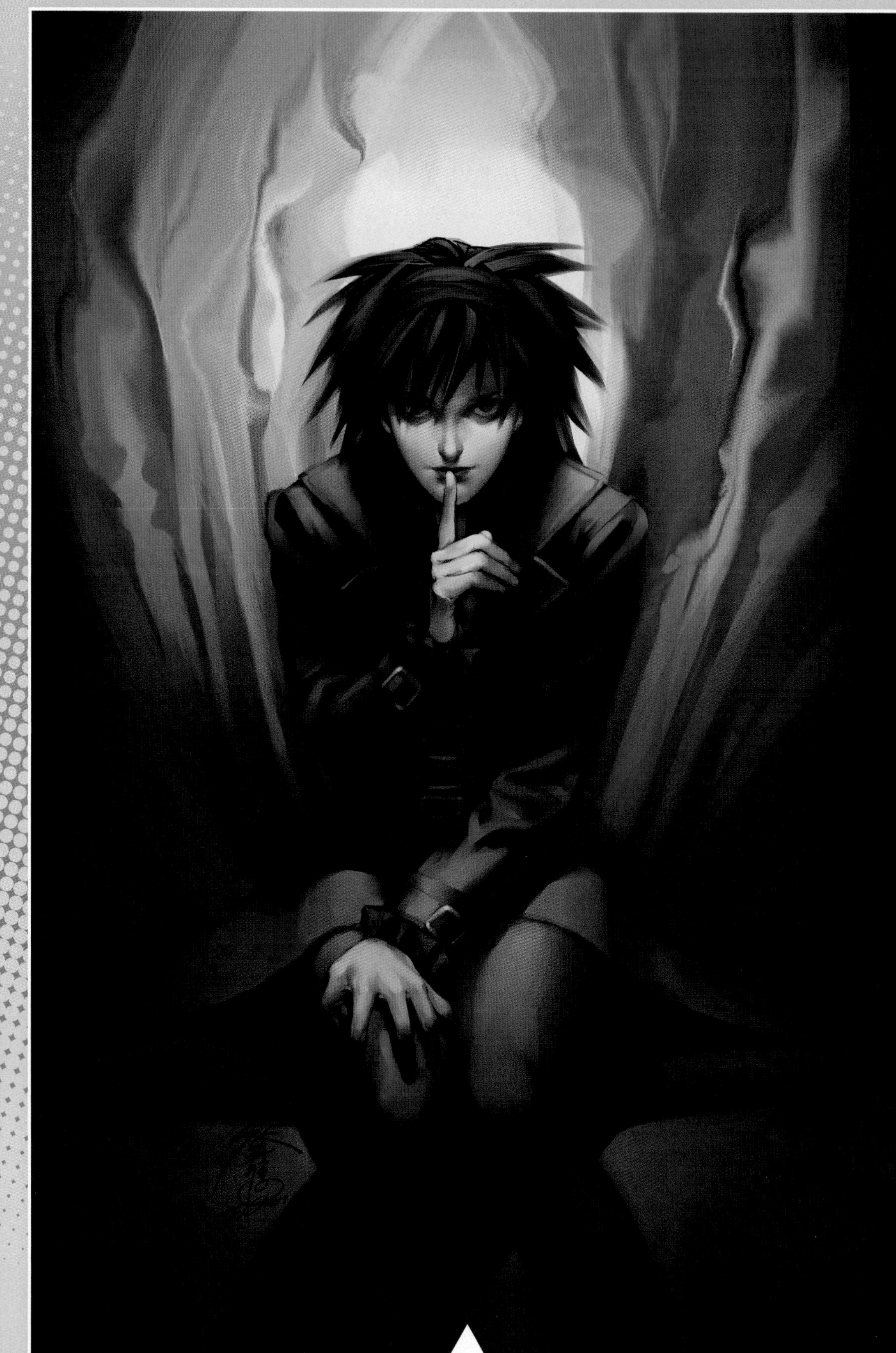

Daredevil, what's the sit-rep?
If we don't find a way to put the Hulk down fast, he's gonna tear right through the *White House!*

It's Spider-Man, Cap, he's... he's *dead!*
Don't worry, gentlemen, *I* can handle this!

After all, there's more than one way to soothe a savage beast.

Okay, wait. Time out for a second.
This is totally retarded.

What?
First of all, you're not part of this mission. And second, you're, like... horrifically out of character.
Hulk *smooch!*

You're supposed to be the Invisible Woman, not *Mrs. Skank-tastic.*
You don't know what you're talking about, dude. My older brother *interned* for the Fantastic Four last year. He said Sue Richards hits on anything that moves.

And just so you know, it's not cool to use "retarded" in a pejorative manner. My cousin's girlfriend is a retard.

Hey, can you, um... send me that skin?

All right, this campaign is obviously a bust, so--

Alex Wilder, get off that thing *now!*

Sorry, boys...

# PRIDE and JOY

BLAHZAY
STARK
SPIDEY
INV. WOMAN
...the overlords beckon.

What in God's name have you been doing in here all day? Is that *pornography?*
*No,* Mom, it's an M.M.O.R.P.G.
STARK

What the hell is that?
A massively multi-player...
*sigh* It's a game, *Dad.* Like *Scrabble,* but for the computer, you know?
Does it cost me money?

Well, yeah, but you got it for me as a birthday gift!
You turned sixteen *months* ago, Alex. I wasn't paying for a lifetime sub-scription.
BRUCE!
But it's the only place I can hang out with my friends!

Besides, we live in *Malibu!*

What difference does a few dollars make?

STARK

We're able to afford a home here, young man, because *my* father taught me that *every* dollar makes a difference.

Then let me get a job! Please! I could--

Cancel the service. *Today.*

Yes, sir.

BRUCE!

I know you think I'm a monster, Alex, but someday you'll understand that everything I did was done out of love.

And when that day comes... I hope you remember to put your mother and me in a decent *nursing home.*

EASY★STAR
For now, I would appreciate it if you'd simply change into something *clean.*
Our guests will be here at seven.

Jeez, he's in a mood.
I'm sorry, honey, but you know how nervous he gets before these things.
I don't understand why. Every year, you guys just invite the same five couples over to sip brandy and cut checks.
When other people in L.A. do charity events, they put on, you know, celebrity golf tournaments... fun stuff.
EASY ★ STAR
Alex, your father and I have told you, good deeds should be done in secret, with no expectation of reward. It's what makes us human.
Yeah, I know. I just wish I didn't have to babysit your friends' creepy kids while you guys get to hide in the library.
We're not hiding. We're doing sensitive work in private. And those five children are anything but "creepy".
Oh, yeah? What about that white guy who always calls me "brother"? Or that dorky girl who still hasn't given me back the Prisoner DVDs I let her borrow last year?
Alex, you're being obnoxious. The six of you have been having nothing but marvelous times together since you were all in diapers.
And unlike your "internet friends", those kids think of you as family. They can't wait to see you!

I don't wanna go!
The Yorkes Residence 6:01 P.M.
If you guys are so obsessed with helping the poor, why won't you let me join the *socialist club*?
Gertrude, as we discussed, while capitalism may be the unequal distribution of wealth, socialism is the equal distribution of *poverty.*
And you're only a sophomore in high school, Gert. There's a reason they call you kids "wise fools".
Actually, that's a *fake* etymology, Dad.
"Sophomore" is derived from "sophist". It has no direct correlation to the Greek word for "fool"... as any *fool* would know.
Do other parents have to deal with this?

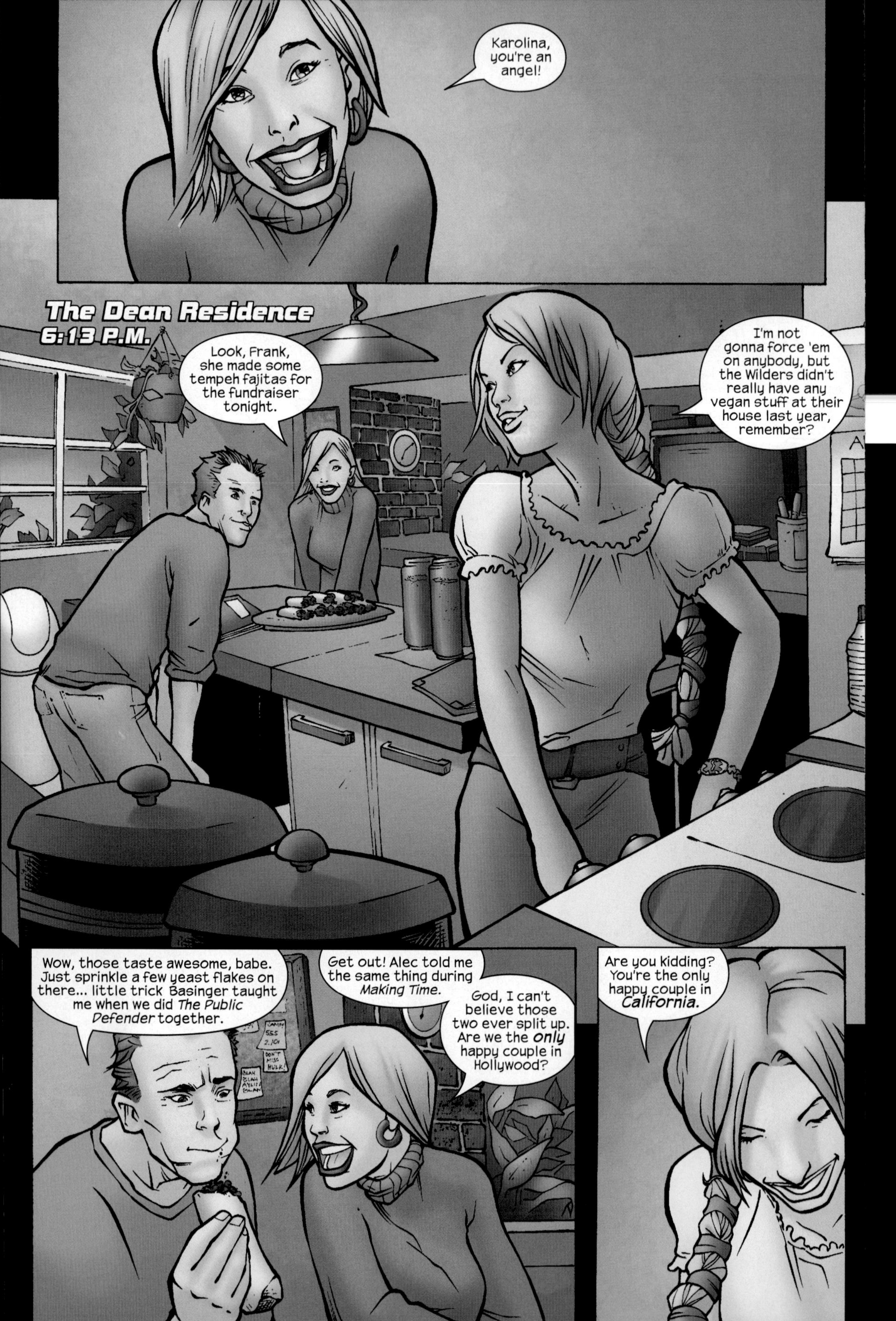

Karolina, you're an angel!
The Dean Residence
6:13 P.M.
Look, Frank, she made some tempeh fajitas for the fundraiser tonight.
I'm not gonna force 'em on anybody, but the Wilders didn't really have any vegan stuff at their house last year, remember?
Wow, those taste awesome, babe. Just sprinkle a few yeast flakes on there... little trick Basinger taught me when we did The Public Defender together.
Get out! Alec told me the same thing during Making Time.
God, I can't believe those two ever split up. Are we the only happy couple in Hollywood?
Are you kidding? You're the only happy couple in California.

UHN!
The Stein Residence
6:22 P.M.
Victor, stop it!
That's for talking back! You think straight C's are funny?
You're becoming a dumb jock, Chase. Is that what you want to be, a cliché?
Well, you're a nerd who punches like a girl... isn't that a cliché?
Keep making jokes, big man. We'll see how hard you're laughing after we pull you off lacrosse.
You wouldn't dare, you little--
That's enough, Chase. Go get dressed. We'll discuss your future on the way to the Wilders.
Groovy, really looking forward to that chat...

Dad, can we talk about my body?
The Hayes Residence
6:37 P.M.
Um, what?
There's, like, all this gross stuff happening. I tried to talk with Mommy about it, but she said to ask you. 'Cause you're a doctor, I guess.
But... so is she!
Well, I can try looking it up on Google or--
No! No, it's good that you came to me, Molly. Let's see, you just turned twelve, so--
Daaaaad! You know I'm still eleven!
Oh. Right.
Actually, Molly, how about if your mother and I both sit down with you... but after the party, okay? I really don't want to be late this year.

We are not going to be late!
The Minoru Residence
6:49 P.M.
Nico, you've been in there for three hours! Let's go!
I can't find my stupid black nail polish!
Oh, sweetie, I threw it away.
What?!
Oprah's doctor friend said that teens who wear black fingernail polish are more likely to do drugs, so I--
Great! Now I have to mix all my old polish together and try to make black!
We're going to be late, aren't we?

The Wilder Residence
7:25 P.M.
Alex, get down here, please!
We have company!
Al-ex! What's happenin', brother?
Hello, Chase.
Sorry we're late, all! Big pile-up on Cliffside.
Alex, you remember our daughter Nico, don't you?
Holy...

Hey, Alex.
I, um, brought your *Prisoner* DVDs back. They were amazing.
PRISONER
They... they *were?*
Completely. "The Chimes of Big Ben" was insane. I can't believe how *old* that show is, you know? Feels like it's from the *future.*
PAYCE!

You okay? You're acting all Keanu.

No, it's just, I mean, you look totally... *different.*

If you need a date for any of your formals or stuff, I get a discount from this limo company that my friend--

Nico!

God, you are ***so hot.*** Where'd you get that outfit?

Oh, thanks, Karolina. Actually, I *made* it...

Gert, can I ask you a question about girl stuff?

Under no circumstances.

Well, now that we're all here, I believe the adults will be retiring to the *library* for a few hours.

Why don't you kids hang out in the game room for a bit?

I'm sure you've got a lot of catching up to do.

OH BOY!
BUSTIN' CAPS
HOOD RAT
PADDLIN'
RACING IS FUN
Yawn
What she said.
Listen, I know we'd all rather be somewhere else right now, but we're stuck here for at least another hour, so we might as well *try* to amuse ourselves.
So what's the plan, man?
Please be beer, please be beer, please be beer...
Hee.
Let's spy on the 'rents.

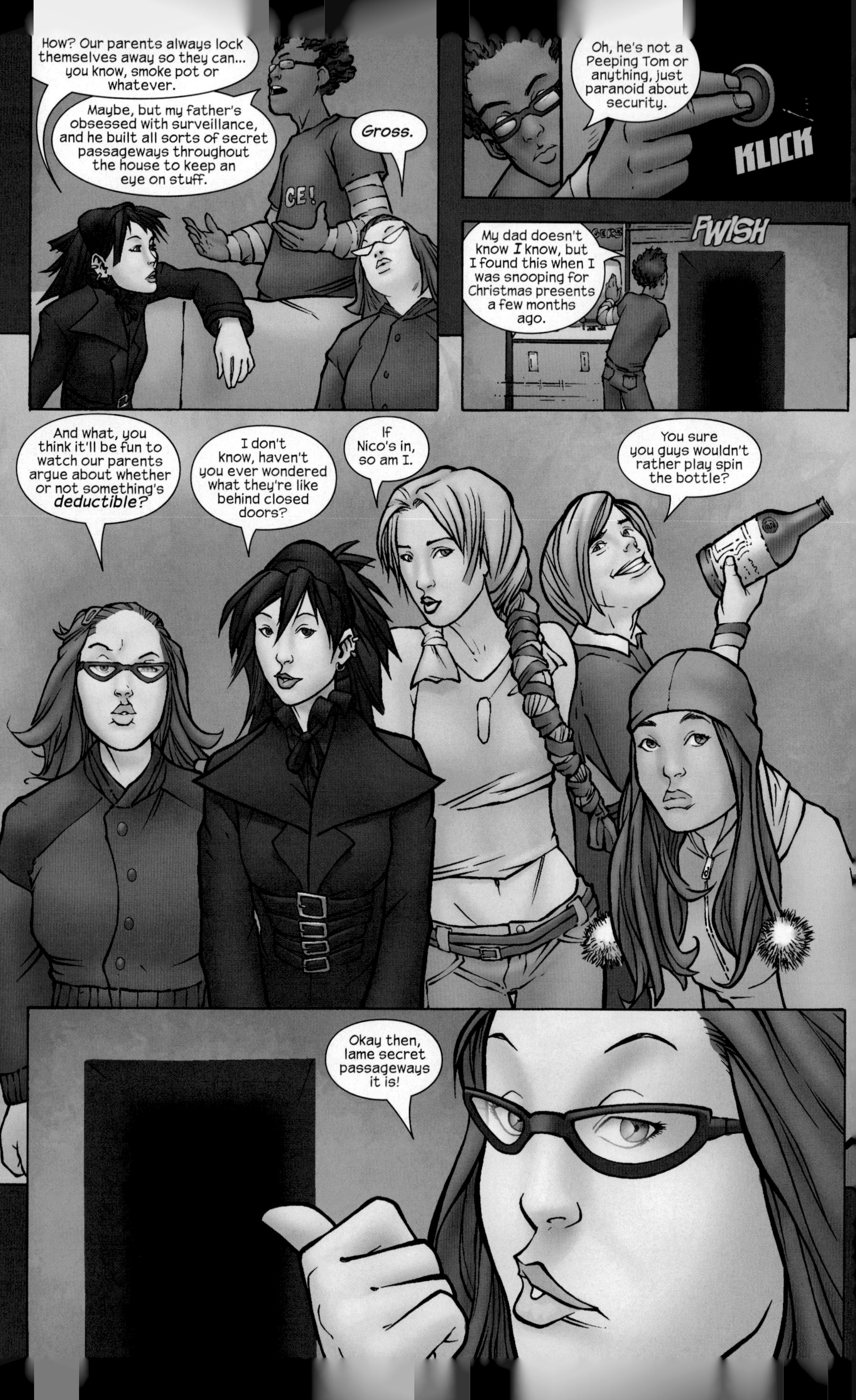
How? Our parents always lock themselves away so they can... you know, smoke pot or whatever.
Maybe, but my father's obsessed with surveillance, and he built all sorts of secret passageways throughout the house to keep an eye on stuff.
Gross.
CE!
Oh, he's not a Peeping Tom or anything, just paranoid about security.
KLICK
FWISH
My dad doesn't know *I* know, but I found this when I was snooping for Christmas presents a few months ago.
And what, you think it'll be fun to watch our parents argue about whether or not something's *deductible*?
I don't know, haven't you ever wondered what they're like behind closed doors?
If Nico's in, so am I.
You sure you guys wouldn't rather play spin the bottle?
Okay then, lame secret passageways it is!

The Corridors
9:15 P.M.
This is like the haunted mansion at Disney... only boringer.
Quiet, Molly. I'm pretty sure these walls are soundproof, but I don't want to take any chances.
What about these windows, bro? Won't they be able to see us?
No, they're actually one-way mirrors.
Or is that *two-way*? I always forget...
Can I hold onto you, Alex? My night vision stinks.
Uh, yeah, sure.
I think we're almost at the library, so keep your eyes peeled for--
What the...?
Very well, ladies and gentlemen...

...if we're all satisfied with Mr. and Mrs. Dean's plans for our off-world enemies, I suggest we move on to The Pride's final order of business.

Is... is that my *mom and dad?*
"The Pride"?
Check out those costumes.
Are you guys thinking what I'm thinking?
PAYCE
Yeah, our parents are totally *gay.*
PAYCE
No... they're *super heroes.*

Dear, would you bring out our guest of honor, please?

With pleasure, love.

Whoa, who's the *piece?*
Okay, this is starting to get a little *Eyes Wide Shut*...

Karolina, I think you better take Molly back to the game room. **Now.**
But I wanna see the super heroes!
Um, sure, Alex. Come on, Miss Molly, the grown-ups are just putting on a stupid play. Let's go fix your hair.
What's wrong with it...?

Is that a *working girl,* Wilder? I thought you and your wife only handled drugs and gambling in this town.
Local matters are none of your concern, Yorkes. I don't question what you two do in the Fourth Dimension, do I?
Did... did he say *drugs?*
Alex, what if they're *not* good guys?
PAYC
Well, *duh.* I've known our parents were evil since I was *five.* This perverted little gathering just confirms it.
Relax, you two. We still don't know anything. Maybe that girl is some *runaway* they rescued...
Speak for yourself, freak. My folks are practically *saints.*

Dr. Hayes, will you and your husband kindly restrain the girl?
Already on it.
*Nnn!* What are you--
Does your machine need time to charge, Stein?
It runs on a self-replicating string of unstable molecules. We're ready when you are.
Then the floor is yours, Mr. Minoru.
*"Antin krek varin..."*
Don't worry, Nico, they're using their real names.
If they were villains, they'd be calling each other stuff like Red Skull and... and *Electro.*

I want you to know that you're helping us forge a better tomorrow for our children.
"Vriik hr Nisanti..."
"Nisanti hr karinn!"
On behalf of everyone in The Pride, we truly appreciate your sacrifice.
Wait, you said no--
SHUNK
Welcome, friends, to the end of the world as we--
Aieeeee--

What the hell was that?
MOON SHYNE

The Wilder Residen e.
9:47 P.M.
That noise.
Sounded like *screaming.*

The catacombs.
Catacombs? You said this place was secure, Wilder!
As if you don't have secret passageways in your lair, Minoru.
Relax, boys. It was probably just psychic residue from the sacrifice.
Regardless, I want that worthless husk disposed of immediately.
Frank, Leslie, sweep the tunnels for rats.
Dear, you'd better check on the children.

God help us if those kids saw what we did.
We always knew they'd find out sooner or later, Hayes.
But they're not *ready* to know about The Pride! We're supposed to protect them from all this until they're *eighteen.*
It's what the Abstract dictates!
There's no cause for alarm, ladies.
I'm sure our young ones are *fine.*

Upstairs. 9:51 P.M.
AHHHH!
Alex?
Stop it!
Get off!
You're hurting me!
Alex, what is going *on* in--
Oh, hey, Mom.

Alex, is... is everything all right up here?
Uh, yeah, totally. We were just fooling around with one of *your* old games.
And you think *Vice City* is dirty.

Why? Is everything all right with *you?*
Of course. It's just, we heard yelling, and we were afraid...

Well, I'm glad you're all *okay.*
Anyway, your parents and I are almost done with the last draft of the new fundraising charter. We'll be up in a few.
Try not to break anything *expensive* before then?

Heh, not a problem, Mrs. W.
PAYCE

SLAM
whew
I have never run... so fast... in *my life.*
Do you think she bought it, Alex?
I don't know. I... I think I'm gonna puke.
PAYCE

Okay, will someone *please* tell me what's going on? What did I miss down there?
Why'd we stop Twistering? We just started!

Gert, take Molly to the bathroom or something.
Why?
BLA
WL
BI
1 BAD MUTHA
DANCE!

So we can fill Karolina in on what happened, okay?
But this involves *Molly's* parents, too! She deserves to know the truth!
She's just a kid!
She's old enough to know her parents are *evil!*

Um, *helloooo.*
I *know* what you guys are whispering about...

You... you do?
Duh.
S... E... X. I'm not a *baby*.

Fine.
Come on, kid. Let's go powder our noses.
That's code for *pee,* right?

What the heck is going on, guys? You're scaring me.
Karolina, you... you better sit down. I don't know how to tell you this, but--
Alex's dad just killed some chick.
1 BAD MUTHA

Chase!
Huh?
BLA
WHAT?

It wasn't just *my dad!* It was all of our parents! You *saw!*
We have no clue *what* we saw, dude!
They stabbed an innocent girl in the *heart!*

Stabbed?
Well, we don't *know* she was innocent... right?

Are you guys *high?*
Our parents are *super-villains!*

Actually, I think he might be right, Karolina.
You mean, like... like Doctor Doom?
Yeah, only times twelve. They said they were part of something called "The Pride".
Whoever they are, we have to... to stop them.
How? You expect us to get a few shotguns and go all Menendez brothers on 'em?
We can't exactly confront them, can we? How do we know they won't kill us?
Battle stations, kiddies.
Something wicked this way comes.

Hey, gang!
Don't worry, the old-timers are finally packing it in for the night.
Gertrude, could I get some of your strapping male friends to give us a hand taking this out to the car?
I guess. What's in that thing?
Oh, you know, just some antiques the Wilders were nice enough to donate for our auction next month.
Um, Nico and I can get that, Mr. Yorkes.
Yeah, uh, I may not be one of the boys, but playing tuba in the marching band has given me amazing upper-body strength.
Remember to lift with your knees, sweetie.
Yes, we don't want anyone getting *hurt* tonight.

Oh, my God... is this what I *think* it is?
Maybe. Feels about right, doesn't it?
*Nothing* feels right, Alex!
Do you think *they* know that *we* know?
Would they let us carry this if they did?

So what? Are we supposed to go home and act like *nothing happened*?
For now, just so our parents don't get suspicious.
But I'll get everybody's e-mail addies before they take off. We can all meet up later tonight, figure out what to do next.
PAYCE!
Right.
What to do next...

The Griffith Observatory. 1:03 A.M.
Hey, Short Bus, why didn't you just say meet at the planetarium?
It took me an hour to figure out where this stupid James Dean memorial was.
Sorry, Chase. That was my suggestion. The planetarium's pretty much the same distance from all of our houses.
JAMES DEAN
Oh, no, it... it was a great idea, Karolina. I'm just messin' with you.
I don't know why Nico's not here yet. She replied to the forward, right? You don't think she--
I'm here, I'm here!
Sorry, Gert doesn't have her permit yet, so I had to give her a ride.
And I lost my stupid glasses, so we had to stop and pick up contact solution and--

Whatever. Everyone was able to sneak out okay?
Yeah, my parents were practically unconscious. Satanic rituals must really wear a person down.
I still feel bad leaving Molly out of the loop. I hope she's... you know.
Is anyone else having a hard time processing this?
I mean, no matter what you guys saw down there, it sounds like our parents have been leading some kind of freaky double lives... for *years,* probably. How is that *possible?*
What? How is it possible that our parents *lied* to us?
Let's see: Santa, the Tooth Fairy, the Easter Bunny, um, ***God.***
"You're the prettiest kid in school. This won't hurt a bit. Your face will freeze like that..."
"Everything's going to be all right."

So what do we do now?
Well, whatever it is, we should decide as a group.
But I say we call the cops. They can take our parents to the Vault, or wherever they hold the Sinister Six-types these days.
Alex, if this Pride really is a group of... of "bad guys" like you think it is, how come I never read about them in my History of Masked Crime elective?
I couldn't even find anything about them on the Internet.
Exactly. Just 'cause they dress up in stupid outfits doesn't make them super-terrorists or whatever.
It's called a secret society, boys and girls. Like the Freemasons? Am I the only one who saw From Hell?
But if I accuse my mom and dad of something, and it turns out they didn't really do it, it could still ruin their careers. That happens all the time in Hollywood.
Yeah, the more I think about it, the more I realize it was probably just some kind of lame performance piece. We should forget we ever saw it and go back to our lives.
Jeez, live in denial much, Chase? I say we get LAPD on the horn and narc these psychos out.
I agree... which means we're two for and two against.
You're the tiebreaker, Nico.

God, I... I don't know.
We're talking about our ***parents.*** Mine aren't perfect, but they're not ***monsters.*** They never were to me, anyway.
But I keep thinking about that ***girl.*** She wasn't much older than us, you know? If nothing else, we should try to get to the bottom of this for her.
So I guess I say... make the call.
Weak!
You're just voting that way 'cause you wanna suck face with Alex.
I do not!
I mean--
Forget it, Nico. Paul, a little dialing music...
You're making a big mistake, bro.

Parker Center, Headquarters of the Los Angeles Police Department. 1:07 A.M.

BRRIING

POLICE DEPT.

Homicide Two, Douglas.

Hi, I'd, um, like to report a murder. I mean, I wouldn't *like* to, but--

Slow down, son. What happened?

Well, that's sorta... *complicated.* You gotta understand, we're not talking about a couple of gang-bangers doing a drive-by here.
Uh-huh. And what *are* we talking about?
My parents. And their friends. They're part of *The Pride.* They're, like, dark wizards and... and mad scientists, and--

Nice try, kid.
That line might work in New York, but it's gonna take a lot more than that for *us* to lock up your folks.

No!
God, please, I swear I'm not lying!

Listen, even *if* you're telling the truth--which seventeen years on the job tells me you're clearly *not*--meta-crime isn't our jurisdiction.
Try the super-freaks in Manhattan. I think the Avengers got some kinda hotline.

No kidding. I've been calling it since I was *eight!* It's just a machine! And they don't respond to anything unless it's, like, a full-scale alien invasion!
Besides, by the time Captain America checks his voicemail, our parents will probably have butchered a *dozen* other--
KLICK

Told you.

Guess we're on our own.
We can't just give up! The police will *have* to believe us if we bring them some kinda evidence.

Like what, one of our parents' Halloween masks?
No, more like a *body.*
Exactly. Where's the trunk now?

Trunk? *What* trunk?
Why does it always feel like I accidentally skipped a chapter?
Gert's dad probably already dumped it into the *tar pits* or something, Nico.

Actually, he and my mom carried it inside as soon as we got home.
And you think it's still there? With the... the *girl* in it?

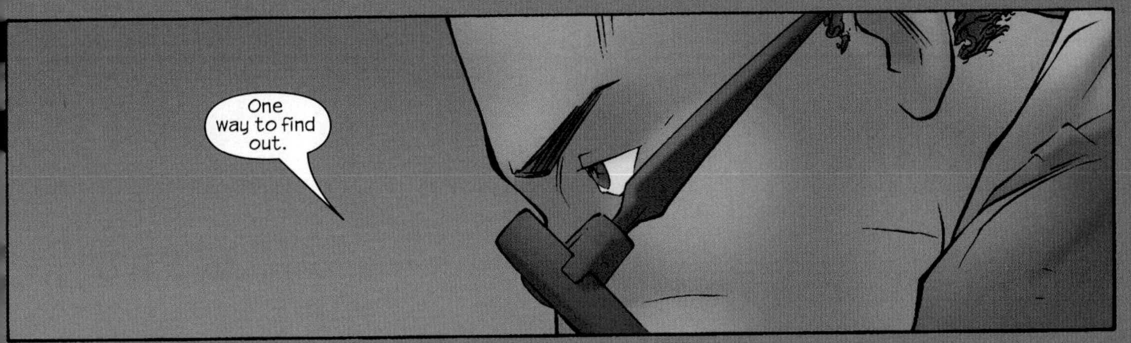
One way to find out.

Santa Monica Freeway. 1:59 A.M.
I ran away from home, and now I'm running *back* there?
This is purely smash-and-grab, Gert. We'll be in and out.
Please don't say In-N-Out. I'd *kill* for one of their burgers right about now. I've got this thing with stress and *food...*
I still think we should have taken my car. It's less conspicuous than the Shaggin' Wagon here.
Hardly. Remember those two sniper dudes last year? When everyone in Virginia was looking for one white van?
The cops couldn't find it 'cause every plumber and electrician and whatever drives one of these things. They're everywhere.
That's why I asked my parents for one.
I get in this bad boy, and I totally drop off The Man's radar.
Okay, is anyone else worried that some of the fruit didn't fall far enough away from the tree?

The Yorkes Residence. 2:43 A.M.
All right, keep the volume on low. We don't wanna wake the big bads.
Don't worry, my parents slept through the '94 earthquake.
Plus, they bought practically the only house in California with a basement in it so I could play drums without ticking off the neighbors.
Wow, it's like a whole season of Antiques Roadshow down here. How are we gonna find anything?
Well, at least I found my accursed glasses. Granted, they were in my pocket...
What if there's a secret passage or something? Like in Alex's house?
But no sign of that pirate chest. See, no evidence of nothing.
Check around for some kind of switch...
D. GLITZ CAMERA CO.

Hey, here's one of those security keypad things.
Don't touch it! You'll probably set off sirens and stuff!

Looks like we need a five-digit password, something with the numbers three, four and seven.
How can you tell?
Those keys are a *smidge* darker than the other ones, from the oil on your fingertips, you know?

Get out! That is so *C.S.I.,* Nico!
Are there letters with the numbers?
Yeah, like on a phone. Why? What can you spell with those three digits?

Pride.

The name of their little club? Isn't that sorta *obvious?*
Well, my mom's AOL password is *"password"*. Old people aren't exactly good at this stuff.
It's not worth the risk, Alex! If my parents catch us down here, we're dead. *Literally.*
I know I said they were heavy sleepers, but they're not--
Try it, Nico. I've got a feeling about this.
Have a little faith in me.
BEEP BEEP BEEP BEEP BEEP
I do, Alex.
I--
FWISH
Whoa!
A trapdoor? Are you *kidding* me?
It worked! It actually--

HSSSSSSSSS

The Yorkes Residence
2:49 A.M.
HSSSS

What the %@#*?!

Nobody move! They... they can only sense motion.
What do you mean *"they"*? What is it?!
That thing from ***Jurassic Park.*** A... A ***Velociraptor.***

That's impossible, Alex! They're not--
***Ahh,*** get it away!

***Chill,*** Karolina. It's gotta be C.G.I. or whatever. I'll prove it.
Chase...
***Don't!***
***Put it down!***
You're gonna get us ***killed!***

Look, it's nothing but...
KRAK
RRRRR
Oh.
ROARR

STOP IT!
RRR?
"...art in Heaven... hallowed be Thy name..."
Down, girl.
Hh... heel.
RRRRRR

How... how did you...?
I have no idea.

What the hell just happened?!
Is... Is this a dream?
We have to go. Now!

Quiet, we're gonna wake Gert's psycho parents.
I can't deal with them and a... a whatever that thing is.
It's okay, Alex. I told you, my folks sleep like the dead, and they're three floors up. They can't hear a--

Hello, Gertrude.

Mom?
Dad?
Everybody, run! I'll try to hold them--
--off?
Wait, the dinosaur is real, but her parents are C.G.I.?
No, I... I think those are holograms.
Hey, squirt. I'm sorry, but if you're watching this projection we recorded... your mother and I are probably dead.
What?

Hopefully, we were able to get this secret chamber's access code to you before we died.
Don't be absurd, Stacey. If we didn't get her the code, how would she be watching us now? You think she just *accidentally* stumbled into all of this?
Well *actually*...
Presumably, you've already met your *"pet"*.
Don't be scared, she doesn't bite... unless there's someone you *want* her to bite, of course.
Before our 4-D time portico was destroyed, we traveled to the 87th century and had her commissioned. Cost us a pretty doubloon, so I hope you're grateful.
She's been genetically engineered to respond to only *your* mental commands. She'll protect you from whichever self-righteous do-gooder finally managed to kill us.
Hold up, the *which* century?
I'm sure you have lots of questions, but you'll find all the answers you're looking for inside our *Abstract*, the sacred text that guides our organization.
It will explain everything we've ever done, and everything *you* need to do now that we're gone.

Is this a joke? It's written in some foreign language.
It may seem like gibberish now, but it will all make perfect sense once you've deciphered the text.
Just use the decoder ring Mr. and Mrs. Dean gave you when you turned eighteen.
My parents gave you a ring?
No, and I'm only fifteen! I don't know what they're talking about!
You may need help with this adjustment period, so seek out whichever members of The Pride are still alive. They're your family now.
You've always known the world was being run into the ground by a bunch of brainless cowards, but the future belongs to great minds like you...
...so steal tomorrow from them and make it your own.
Okay, um... huh?
So can we go to the police now? Please?
With what? We've got Gert's parents claiming they're some kind of time travelers, but we still don't have any evidence that they helped kill that girl.
Are you nuts? They've got psychic raptors in their basement!

And Siegfried and Roy have *white tigers* in theirs. Doesn't mean they're criminals, just means they're... *odd.*
Gert's right. This definitely proves we're onto something huge, but we still need a smoking gun to put our parents away for good.
Without it, they'll probably just Shapiro their way out of jail and kill us as soon as they're free.
What about that not-so-little black book of theirs? Didn't they say it's got info on all of their crimes and stuff? Maybe it says where they hid the girl's body.
And all we have to do is decipher the thing, right? So let's go to Karolina's house and look for that magic decrypto ring.
*My* house? But... but my parents can't *really* be part of this. They might be a little eccentric, but they're not *evil*. They don't even eat *meat!*
Well, neither did *Hitler.*
Karolina, if you'd seen what the rest of us saw back at my house, you'd understand. I'm with Nico. We should press on to your pad next.
But first, we have to figure out what to do with this... thing. Gert's parents said it's supposed to protect her, but they're not exactly *trustworthy*. Besides, the five of us are conspicuous enough as is.
Sorry, girl. Guess that means it's back in the doghouse for you. But don't worry, once this is all over, I promise to come back for you, okay?
HSSSS
I thought my life was weird *yesterday*...

Ventura Freeway
3:38 A.M.
Okay, so I've been thinking...
This oughta be good.
Just listen, all right? I believe you now... our parents aren't part of some dorky D & D club. They're obviously severely screwed up.
But that means we're all in the line of fire. If we keep snooping around our houses, we're probably gonna end up like that chick they whacked.
You have a better plan?
There's this cool place I always go to hang by myself whenever my parents start throwing stuff at each other. I stumbled onto it a few years ago.
It's totally abandoned and pretty much impossible to find. We should go there and, you know... lay low until this thing blows over.
It's never gonna "blow over", Chase! Our parents have probably been doing horrible stuff since before we were born, and nobody knows about it.
It's up to us to tell the world what they've done. We can't just hide in your little clubhouse and... and wait for somebody to do it for us!

It's not a clubhouse, you condescending piece of--
Settle, Chase.
I understand why you're nervous, but you don't have to worry about my place. My parents are totally cool. Besides, they're not even home.
They're not?
They had to catch the red-eye to New York after your parents' party last night. My mom said that they're doing a reading of some Broadway play tomorrow.
Sure, but after all this, who knows what they're really up to.
Well, all I know is that they're gone.
Wait, your mom and dad go out of town and let you stay home by yourself?
Man, you are so lucky!

Making any headway with that, Sherlock?
Hardly. It's tougher than the Saturday crossword.
You all right, Gert?
Yeah, just thinking about the last animal my parents let me have. It was this Vietnamese pot-bellied pig named Orwell. I loved that stupid thing, but my parents hated it.
A few years ago, I was playing with him in the backyard, right? I ran in to answer the phone for a second, and when I came out, he was gone. Never saw him again.
Aw, that sucks.
My mom and dad said I left the gate open, but that's a total lie. They probably went all Lord of the Flies on him as soon as I turned my back.
From that moment on, I swore never to trust my parents again. It was so obvious they weren't telling the truth...
I mean, I know I locked that gate!

The Dean Residence
4:14 A.M.

This room's clean.
Any luck up there, Karolina?

Nope, and Nico and I have been through every jewelry box and trinket drawer in the house.
No offense, but I seriously don't think my parents are like the rest of yours. They're *good people.*
Although her mom does have more shoes than an entire season of *Cribs*...

Well, keep looking for some kind of switch or keypad thing. There's gotta be a trapdoor around here somewhere.
Why? Just because our houses were tricked out doesn't mean *this* place is.

Never fear, kiddies. Chase is on the case... and he just hit paydirt.

You found the ring?
Nope, but I was rummaging through Mr. Dean's den, and I scored his last will and testament.
What does that have to do with anything?
Well, that's basically what we found at Gert's place, right? Instructions on what she's supposed to do after her parents kick the bucket?
He's got a point, Alex. That is where we got our last lead.
Hey, that's private!
Relax, looks pretty boring. They didn't leave you any dinosaurs or anything. "We, Frank and Leslie Dean, being of sound mind, blah blah blah."
But check out this last page.
"And to our beloved daughter Karolina, we bequeath the following, may she use it wisely."
And then there's just a picture of this.

That's the caduceus. It's a symbol for--
Yeah, yeah, we've all been to a hospital before, showoff. But why's it got the Ghostbusters symbol around it?
I... I don't know, but that snake thing's engraved on my MedAlert bracelet.
Maybe your parents were trying to tell you not to wear it anymore?
Why? I've had this thing on since I was four. My parents told me never to take it off. I'm, like, deathly allergic to penicillin.
Why would they lie about something like that?
Do you know you're allergic to penicillin, or is that just what your parents said?
I'm not sure, Karolina, but if you want to prove us wrong... just take off the bracelet.
You're crazy! This picture is probably just their way of saying that... that they didn't want me to go to med school!
Parents who don't want their kid to be a doctor? Now that's crazy.

Fine!
If you want it so bad, **have** it! It's ***nothing!***
See?!

Oh no.
It's beautiful. Like... like a burning painting or--
Get away!
What's wrong with me? What am I?
An angel.
A... A mutant, maybe?
She can't be. I mean, not that there's anything wrong with that, but... but she's too old to just turn into one now, isn't she?
Hold on, let me think. Before they sacrificed that girl, didn't my father say something about Karolina's parents dealing with... with "off-world" enemies?
What if your mom and dad, you know, aren't from around here?
What are you...?
You think I'm an alien?

Maybe being on this planet gives your parents and you these... these powers, but something in your bracelet *inhibits* those abilities, sorta like Kryptoni--
You've been watching too many WB shows, bro. That's *ridiculous.*
Are aliens really any harder to accept than *time travelers?*
Besides, it makes sense that your parents would try to suppress your natural talents. It's what parents have been doing since the beginning of *time.*
So I'm the daughter of some kind of, what... *space invaders?* God, first you tell me my parents are *evil,* and now I find out I'm... I'm not even *human?*
...I can fly?
I wish we'd never learned about any of this! I was much happier being kept in the *dark!* I... I hope our parents *do* kill us now! I... I...

Oh, my God!
I CAN FLY!

Parker Center, Headquarters of the Los Angeles Police Department. 4:19A.M.
You summoned, Lieutenant Flores?
Yeah, come in, Douglas. Shut it behind you, will ya?
Don't worry, you're not in any trouble. I just wanted to hear about this crank you got earlier.
LIEUTENANT FLORES
Ah, it was nothing, L.T. This kid called in and tried to convince me his mom and dad were some kinda super-villains.
I get a couple of those every time report cards come out.
Funny.
Yeah, he said they call themselves one of the deadly sins... Pride, I think. Kid's obviously seen Seven too many times.
Well, if that's the caliber of calls we're getting tonight, why don't you punch out early? You've been double-shifting it all week.
Seriously? Thanks, Lieutenant.
You're a prince!

The Wilder Residence
4:21 A.M.

BRRING

Do you have *any idea* what time it is?

It's four in the morning, Mr. Wilder. "Do you know where your children are?"
Lieutenant Flores?

Sorry to bother you, sire... but I think we might have a *problem.*

The Wilder Residence
4:25 A.M.
Alex?
You asleep, pal?
THING
TO
BREAK
NECK.
OOH WEE...
ELEVATE

Geoffrey, put that down!
I'm not going to hurt him, dear. I just want to explain what he saw us doing with this thing. The "sacrifice" Alex thinks he witnessed was nothing but an...
...illusion?
What is our son doing with a male mannequin head in his room?
How the hell can you be concerned about that?
Alex is somewhere out there, and he knows the truth about us!
Calm yourself. We don't know what he knows. We can still come up with a cover story and--
My minion inside the LAPD said that Alex reported a homicide. He mentioned our group by name!
Then it's time to call the others.
No! If the rest of The Pride find out about this, it will be my head you find under the covers!
Well, we can't keep them in the dark! Without The Pride's help, we'll never find Alex.
Don't forget, he's a prodigy when it comes to logic and... and strategy. He could be anywhere by now!

The Dean Residence
Eleven Miles Away
4:28 A.M.
Ha ha, YEAH!
WHEEEEEEEE!
We are so dead...

Stop messing around, Karolina! Someone's gonna see you!
Don't worry, Alex! Our nearest neighbor is like a million acres awa--
OOF!
Oh, my God! Are you okay, Chase?
Yeah, I'm... I'm great.
Guess I need to log a few more miles up there before I get the hang of this.
What does it feel like, Karolina?
It's totally amazing, Nico. You know how you get butterflies in your stomach when you meet someone you like?
Imagine if those butterflies could flap their wings hard enough to... to lift you right off the ground!

It's almost enough to make me forget I'm some kind of extraterrestrial *freak.*

Um, speaking of which, it's probably time for you to come back down to *earth.*

You want me to wear this *thing* again? But it... it represents everything my parents ever *lied* to me about.

Maybe, but that bracelet also turns off your *lightshow.* And right now, we can't have you floating around like an oversized Tinkerbell.

What do you mean *oversized?*

We need to stay below our parents' radar, Karolina. If you can do all this after a few minutes of practice, think what your ***mom and dad*** can do.

This whole super-villain club of theirs is turning out to be a lot more dangerous than any of us first thought.

Exactly, which is why I think our next move should be to get *Molly.*

I know you wanted to protect her from all this because she's just a little kid, but she's probably safer with *us* than she is in her *house.*

I mean, Molly's folks are part of this psycho Pride thing, too, right?

Gert's got a point, Alex.

Besides, if we keep the truth from Molly, how are we any better than our *parents?*

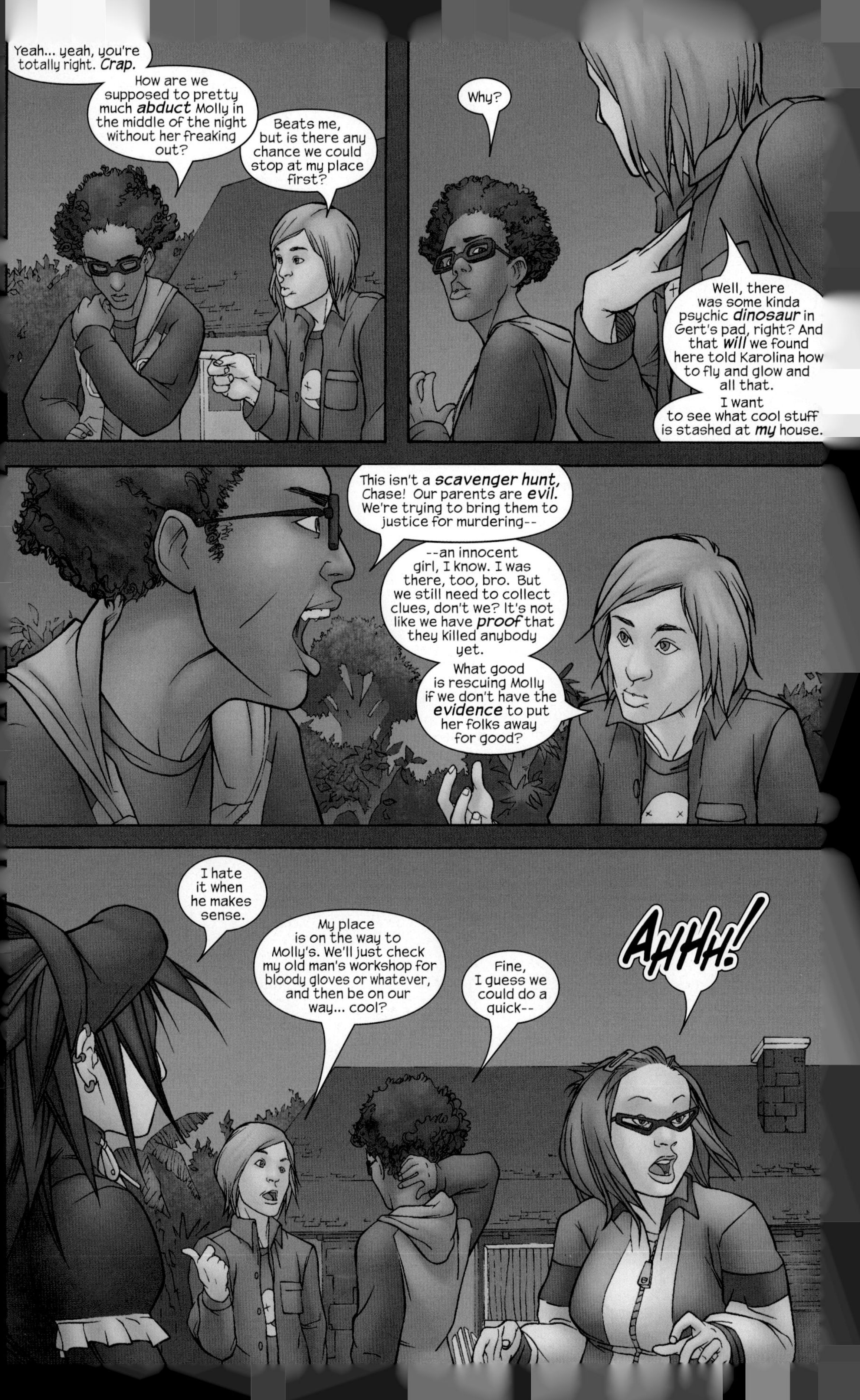
Yeah... yeah, you're totally right. Crap.
How are we supposed to pretty much abduct Molly in the middle of the night without her freaking out?
Beats me, but is there any chance we could stop at my place first?
Why?
Well, there was some kinda psychic dinosaur in Gert's pad, right? And that will we found here told Karolina how to fly and glow and all that.
I want to see what cool stuff is stashed at my house.
This isn't a scavenger hunt, Chase! Our parents are evil. We're trying to bring them to justice for murdering--
--an innocent girl, I know. I was there, too, bro. But we still need to collect clues, don't we? It's not like we have proof that they killed anybody yet.
What good is rescuing Molly if we don't have the evidence to put her folks away for good?
I hate it when he makes sense.
My place is on the way to Molly's. We'll just check my old man's workshop for bloody gloves or whatever, and then be on our way... cool?
Fine, I guess we could do a quick--
AHHH!

What is it, Gert?
Sorry, I... I just got this weird feeling somebody was watching us.
Uh-oh, whenever anyone says that, it always means somebody is.
Relax, guys. I told you, my parents are out of town. And they bought this mansion 'cause it's completely paparazzi-proof. Everything's copacetic.
Well, you can't blame me for being a little Orange Alert here, can you?
Uh-Uh. Let's get to the van and head for the hills.
Beverly Hills, that is.
You gonna be all right?
Not exactly. I'd feel a lot less jumpy if you guys had let me bring my new pet along for protection.
What, that raptor from the future?
No offense, Gert, but that thing didn't exactly make me feel safe...
SSSSSSS

The Stein Residence
4:55 A.M.
Come on, my folks spend most of their time down in this old shed. They know I think their work is insanely boring, so it's probably where they'd hide stuff from me.
No one has a skeleton key on them, do they?
Maybe Karolina could use her *powers* on it?
How? By *bedazzling* it open? Besides, if she de-bracelets, she's gonna light up the backyard like the Century Club.
But what if I focused all of my energy out of a single finger and shot, like, a concentrated beam--
Move.

KLANG
You guys think too much.
Ah, is it just me, or does this place look a lot bigger *inside* than it did *outside?*
Another hologram?
What do your parents *do,* Chase?
They're some kinda engineers. Supposedly, they made a fortune inventing that thing that lets you open up new CDs without ripping your fingernails off.

How did two people so ingenious end up with a son who's so... athletic?
Hey, I may not be book smart, but I am street smart.
Which street? Sesame...?
Check it out!
This stuff is amazing.
Is... is that a piece of brain in there?
Holy...
What is it, Chase?
What do those things do?
Nothing.
Nothing at all.
Take those off this instant, young man.

You are grounded until graduation.
At *least.*
That goes for you, too, Nico.

*Mom? Dad?* What... what are you doing here?
That's exactly what I was about to ask. Alex's mother called us in a panic to see if he was at *our* house. That's when we found out *you* were gone, too.
Your father and I have been scouring all of Los Angeles for you kids. What are you doing in Mr. Stein's workshop? Are... are you making *ecstasy?*

Nevermind. This is a conversation for tomorrow morning.
Right now, you're all going *home.*

Or what, Pop?
You'll use some of your scary *toys* on us?

...he has the Fistigons. If he figures out how to weaponize them--
I didn't want to do this, Chase... but I'm afraid you've forced my hand.
BUDEET DEET
OOF!
What... what just happened?
Did Chase's dad--
Guys, get ready for Tinkerbell!
EHN!

Dammit!
They know about the Dean girl!
We know about *everything,* Mr. Minoru!
We... we know who you people really are!
Oh, I highly doubt *that,* child.

"Nnirak rh itnsin!"

FWOOM

Karolina!

Settle *down,* boy.

THWAP

Why are you *acting* like this, Mom? This *isn't* you! You... you take me to *church* every Sunday!

Faith is a complicated thing, sweetie.

But if you believe anything, believe that this is going to hurt *me* much more than it hurts...

...*you.*

The Staff of One. Her... her body is **absorbing** it.
How...?
What is **wrong** with you, Mom? Snap **out** of it!

SNAP OUT OF IT!

Nico, no!
That's **enough,** young lady!
I'll discipline my **own** child, Victor! You ta care of the Yorkes girl!

helpme helpmehelpme helpme
Help yourself, Gertrude. By coming with **us.**
We have no intention of hurting **any** of you, we just want--

SSSSSSSS
Hm?

RRAAAARRR

AHHHH!
GET IT OFF!
I knew you were out there.

Die, animal!
"VishNin rrK..."

Shut *up*, Dad!
*Don't,* you'll break my--
SPLOOSH
Karolina, your lockpick idea!
Hhh! koff koff koff
Try it against Mr. Minoru!
*What?* That's... that's Nico's *dad.* I can't--
He almost *drowned* you, Karolina! Now *fire!*
Nnnnn!
FZAZZ
AHN!

It worked!
Is... is he all right?
Forget about him, Karolina!
Just get me down from here. Please!
Gert! Control that thing! Those are still Chase's parents!
You heard him, girl.
You don't have to kill the jerks. A slight mauling will do for now.
Uhn.
Nico, gimme a hand with Chase! We have to motor before your mom and dad--
My family.
They're... they're my only family.
I'm sorry, Nico, but we have to let them go. We need to take care of each other now, okay?
Yeah... each other.
Karolina, you have a license, right?
Think you can drive Chase's van?
I... I guess so. As long as it's not a stick shift.

San Bernardino Freeway
5:31 A.M.
MJP
SKREEECH

Sorry! Stupid manual transmission is impossible!
Where am I going, anyway?
The hospital! I've still got a... a giant rod stuck inside my body!

Heh.
Chase?
You're okay...?

Uhn.
Not really. Feels like I finished an entire keg by myself... and then dropped it on my head. And why am I wearing these stupid--
SSSSSSSSS

DAH!
Relax, Chase. She just saved our lives.
I... I thought we locked that thing in your basement!
So did I, but thankfully, she found a way free.
Unless my parents sent her to eat us, of course.
I don't know what you remember, Chase, but your father assaulted you.
Yeah, what else is new? I probably had it coming.
No, you... Regardless, if you're on the mend, and none of our other injuries are life-threatening, I say we scrap Plan A and go straight to the cops, or the press, or--
DEET DA DA DEET DOO
That's messed up.
My cell phone isn't even turned on.
Yello?
Gertrude? Your father and I are very disappointed in you. You have to stop playing these games...

...or I'm afraid we'll have no choice but to do something terrible to your young friend *Molly*.

The Hayes Residence
5:34 A.M.
The call is in.
I told the children that unless they surrender themselves to us within the hour, Molly will be *executed.*

Do you honestly think they'll fall for a *bluff* like that?
Well, if Wilder is right, they've already seen us slay one young girl.

I still can't believe they actually witnessed the *sacrifice.*
Can you imagine what must be going through their minds?
We would've had to tell them about The Pride when they turned eighteen anyway, love. All this does is advance our timetable slightly.

You sure your daughter isn't going to wake up in the middle of this, Doc?
Molly's being telepathically sedated. It's usually pretty effective.
God, I wish *we'd* had mutant powers when *Gertrude* was a baby. If you knew how many sleepless nights she--

Dale, put the samurai battle-axe away, will you? You know how weapons from alternate pasts make me *nervous.*
We need to be ready for anything, dear. These children are young, but that doesn't mean they're--
Mom...?

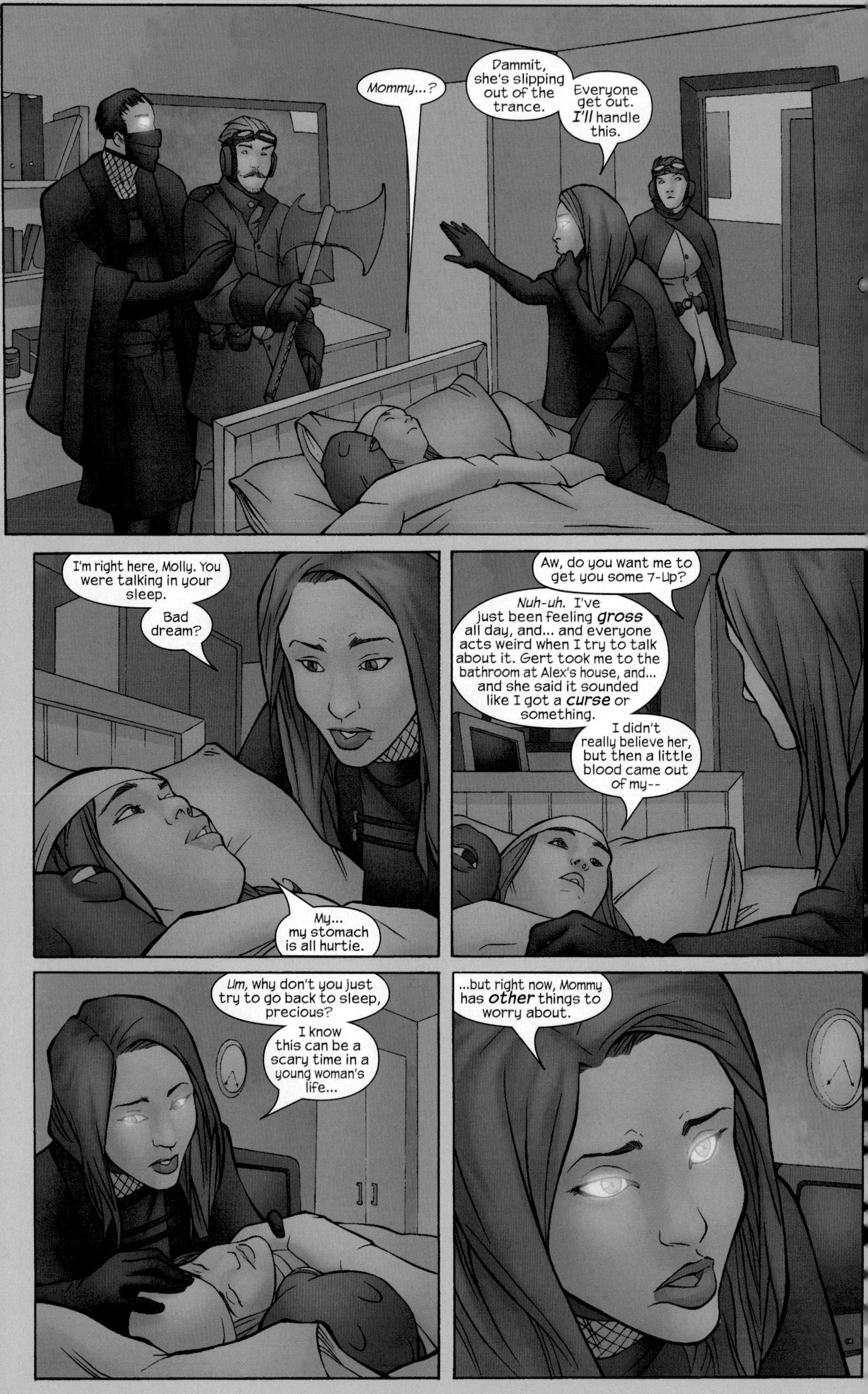

Mommy...?
Dammit, she's slipping out of the trance.
Everyone get out. *I'll* handle this.

I'm right here, Molly. You were talking in your sleep.
Bad dream?
My... my stomach is all hurtie.

Aw, do you want me to get you some 7-Up?
*Nuh-uh.* I've just been feeling ***gross*** all day, and... and everyone acts weird when I try to talk about it. Gert took me to the bathroom at Alex's house, and... and she said it sounded like I got a ***curse*** or something.
I didn't really believe her, but then a little blood came out of my--

*Um,* why don't you just try to go back to sleep, precious?
I know this can be a scary time in a young woman's life...

...but right now, Mommy has ***other*** things to worry about.

Roadside Rest Stop
Closed For Repairs
5:43 A.M.
TOMMY'S
Would they really kill their own daughter?
My mom tried to kill me, Karolina! She stabbed me in the heart with some kind of... of oversized magic wand!
Either way, going to the cops is out. Mommy Dearest specifically said, if we even think about involving the authorities, Molly is dead.
Then what are we supposed to do, just give ourselves up to those psychos?
Maybe there's another option, Karolina.
Exactly. We should go into hardcore hiding, Saddam-style. Like I said, I know this awesome abandoned--
Actually, I was suggesting the opposite of retreat, Chase.
I want to charge into Molly's place and rescue her.

Don't be stupid, Alex! The last time we tried to fight a few of our parents, we barely got out alive!
You don't have to come with me, Gert. None of you do.
*I* was the one who acted like a dumb overprotective brother and wouldn't let Molly come with us, so *I* should be the one who gets her out.
But Alex, you don't even have any *powers.*
It's not like the rest of us do either, Karolina. You're the only one who can float around and zap people.
Yeah, but you've got a psychic man-eating *dinosaur,* Gert. And Chase has, *um*...
A problem! If I can't figure out how to get my dad's stupid geek gloves off, I'm never gonna be able to wipe my own--
FWOOOM
Oh.
Well... *that* totally rocks.

How'd you *do* that, Chase?
Dunno. It just sorta... ***happened.***
In that case, you should probably keep your hands to ***yourself.***

Hey, if Chase can figure out how to use those things, we might actually stand a decent shot against Gert and Molly's parents.
*We?*
So you're coming along, Nico?

We have to take care of each other now... isn't that what you said, Alex?
Well, if *Nico's* in...
Fine, I'm not gonna let you guys stomp my 'rents without me.
Hell, yeah! Pre-dawn raid!

Thanks, guys. If we plan this just right, I know we can get Molly out safely.
I mean, we took down four of our parents once... why can't we do it again?

The Hayes Residence
5:48 A.M.
I took the shuttlecraft back from New York as soon as I heard.

What about Frank, Leslie?
He's stuck in Manhattan, brokering some deal with another intergalactic arms trader. A Skrull, I think... they all look the same to me.
Where are the others?

My wife's upstairs with Molly, and the Wilders are preparing a contingency plan in case the children fail to show.
But the Steins and the Minorus aren't answering their communicators. We're worried that your daughter and the other kids might have *attacked* them.
*Please,* Karolina doesn't have the *spine* for a fight.

And God help any child who's stupid enough to make a move against *us.*

Across The Street
6:26 A.M.
How about you, Delta Team?
You in position, over?
Dude, you're killing the battery on my two-way. For the billionth time, we're all in position and we all remember the plan.
Can we knock off your lame role-playing stuff and do this already?

Ah, roger that, this is Alpha Team, uh... proceeding with Phase One.
We won't all live through this, will we, Alex?

What are you talking about? We're going to be fine, Nico. We just have to stick to the--
People always say teenagers think they're immortal, but I... I don't think that. I mean, all I ever think about is death.
When my mom jammed that staff-thing into my chest, all I could think was... I'm surprised I even lived this long.

I know exactly what you mean.

You do?
Totally. Even before all this.
It's like, every day, the people in charge seem to make the world a little more screwed-up, and we can see it, but there's nothing anyone our age can--

Why... why did you...?
I don't know.
But I do know that talking about it will just ruin it.
Right. 
On to Phase One...

DING DONG
Standby, people!
The prodigal children have returned.
Mr. Wilder, Ms. Minoru... please, come in before someone sees us. I'd hate to have to mind-wipe the neighbors again.
Tell me, where are your other playmates?
Nearby. They'll turn themselves in as soon as we have confirmation that your daughter is safe, Dr. Hayes.
Oh, Alex, just as crafty as your father... always after the quid pro quo.
Unfortunately, that's not how I do business.
KNEEL.
Now tell your friends to show themselves, or I'll force you to snap each other's necks.

Ehn.
Beta Team... Phase... TWO!
Who are you--
KERRASH

AHHHHH!
You guys all right?
Yeah, just make sure your pet keeps the good doctor here occupied.

Nico, you search upstairs, I'll take the--

KRAK!

ALEX!
Girls, I'm *disappointed.*
Call me old-fashioned, but all of this fighting seems very *unladylike.*

Hey, squirt. I see you found your *inheritance.* Funny, last time I checked, your mother and I weren't even *dead* yet.
Yeah, well, you... you *will* be unless you back off, Dad.
You two are *murderers.* I... I have no problem sicking this girl on *you.*

Pretty convincing, Gertrude.
Unfortunately, this creature was genetically engineered to be *incapable* of harming any member of your immediate family.
Now why don't you settle down and--

RAHHH!

No!
AHN!

What did you *do?*
It... it was *instinct!* I didn't mean--

WHEN BLOOD IS SHED... LET THE STAFF OF ONE EMERGE--

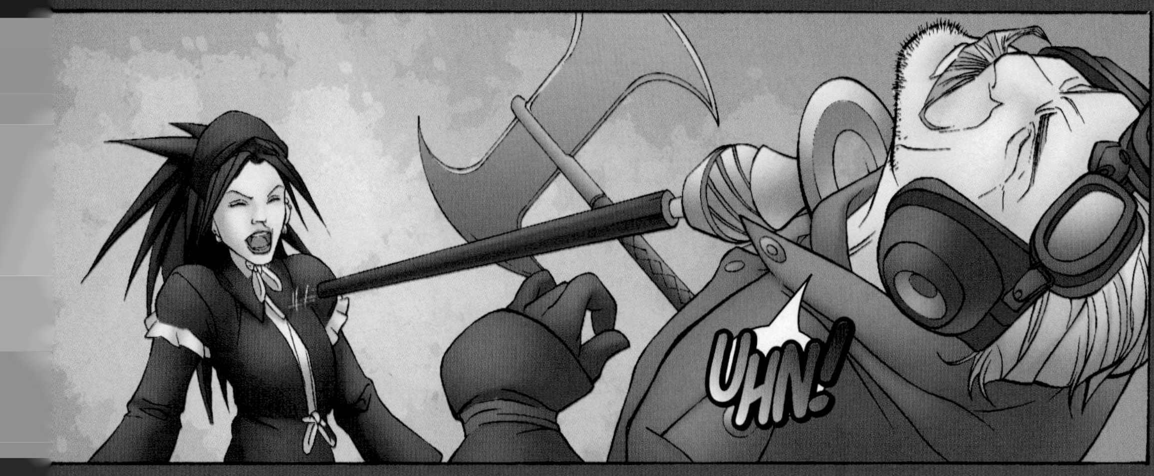
UHN!

Where... where did you get your mother's--

FREEZE.

Nico?
Are... are you *okay*? What did you do to my--
Keep an eye on these people, Gert. And when Alex comes to...

...tell him I'm on to Phase Three.

Let's go, Karolina!
Take off your bracelet and let's storm the castle already!
*Chase,* we're supposed to wait for Alex to signal us with which room Molly's in before we make our move.

Oh, *dude...* I just remembered! These goggles I stole from my dad have some kinda *X-ray vision* in 'em!
Maybe I can use them to look *through* the walls and--
Something tells me this one isn't the *brains* of your operation.

AHHHH!
Hello, my angel.

MOM?!
Stop it! You're... you're hurting him!
Merely detaining him. You'll understand when you learn to use your beautiful gifts, Karolina. I'm just sorry you had to discover them like this.

Your father and I had always hoped to take you to our homeworld before we told you about your unique heritage.
So I... I really am an alien? You and Daddy lied to me?
No, Karolina, we protected you. We gave you what no other girl in Hollywood had... a normal childhood.

And please don't bother taking off that bracelet. You and I have the exact same abilities, and we can't use them to hurt each other.
You made me wear this anchor my entire life!
And if your powers are the same as mine, then... then touching it must do the same thing to you that it does to me.

It must take away everything that makes you special.

Karolina, what are you--

KRACK
AHHHH!

Ouch.

Sorry about that, Chase.
That... that was *incredible,* Karolina! You actually--
Come on, we have work to do.

Hush, little baby, don't say a word. Mama's going to buy you a--
Get your hands off of her, *witch.*

Isn't that the pot calling the *cauldron* black, Nico?
You're the one who looks like she should be burned at the stake.

You... you people are *evil.*
Your generation is all the same.
As soon as you encounter something you don't understand, you label it as *"evil"* and start throwing chairs through Starbucks windows.

Now why don't you drop the big stick and act like an adult?
*Nnngh.* Why don't *you* drop the condescending tone and admit that you're a *monster.*
*Nico?*

What are *you* doing here?

What... what did you *do* to her?
Nothing!
Molly, what *happened*?

Oh, *jeez.*
This is what I was trying to *tell* you...

...something's wrong with my *body.*

Oh, my God. Molly's a... a...?
She *can't* be a mutant. We had her scanned for the X-gene at birth. I thought she was *negative.* I thought--
SHUT UP!
THUNK
Your lies end right--
STOP IT!

GET AWAY FROM MY MOM!

The Hayes Residence
6:40 A.M.
I MEAN IT! LEAVE MY MOM ALONE!

Don't freak, Molly.
I know how scary this must seem, but there's really nothing to be afraid--
SSSSSS
Everything okay up here, Nico?
AIIIEEEE!

A DINOSAUR!
A MUTANT!
Jeez, when Molly said something was happening to her body, I just thought--
No kidding, Gert! That's what we all thought. But we were wrong. And why are you up here? You're supposed to be guarding--
Don't worry, Nico. Chase and Karolina moved into position. They're providing the "parental supervision" and taking care of--
You guys okay?
Alex!
You're all right!
Yeah, but tomorrow morning I'm gonna have a bump the size of--
What are you guys doing in my house?

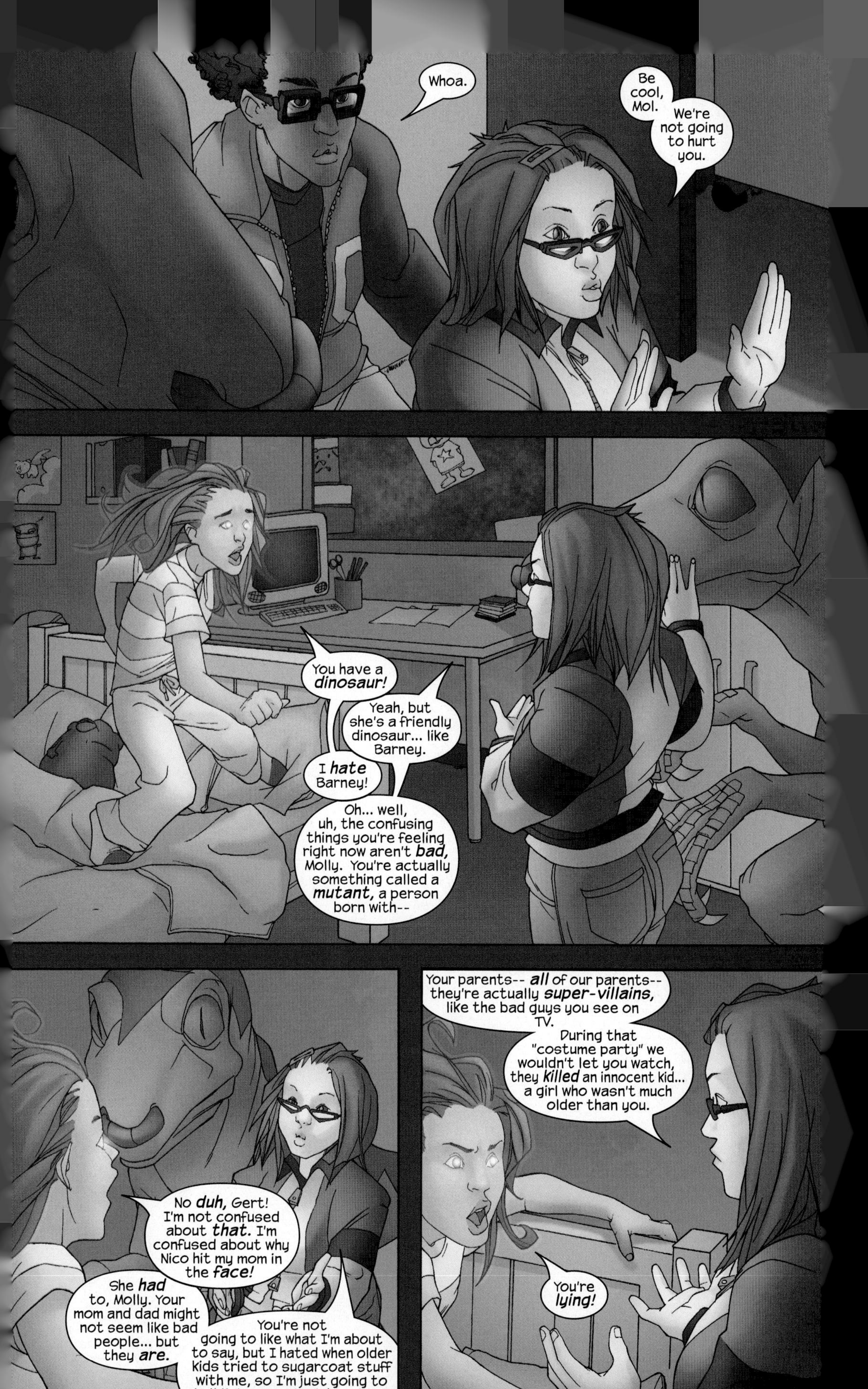
Whoa.
Be cool, Mol.
We're not going to hurt you.
You have a dinosaur!
Yeah, but she's a friendly dinosaur... like Barney.
I hate Barney!
Oh... well, uh, the confusing things you're feeling right now aren't bad, Molly. You're actually something called a mutant, a person born with--
No duh, Gert! I'm not confused about that. I'm confused about why Nico hit my mom in the face!
She had to, Molly. Your mom and dad might not seem like bad people... but they are.
You're not going to like what I'm about to say, but I hated when older kids tried to sugarcoat stuff with me, so I'm just going to tell it to you straight, okay?
Your parents-- all of our parents-- they're actually super-villains, like the bad guys you see on TV.
During that "costume party" we wouldn't let you watch, they killed an innocent kid... a girl who wasn't much older than you.
You're lying!

It's true, little dude. I saw 'em do it.
Chase? Karolina?
If you guys are up here, who's keeping an eye on--
KRooM
I would say that you should have killed me when you had the chance...
...but a chance is the one thing you spoiled brats never had.

Go away, Mom!
Yeah, take one more step and we'll--
Oh, do be quiet, you pudgy little troll woman.
AHHHHHNN!
If any of you move, I'll pop Gertrude here as if she were one of her own blackheads.
I'd rather not kill anyone, but this overweight nerdling was the one child The Pride always considered expendable. The rest of you--
Stop it, Mrs. Dean!
You're hurting her!

Uhf!
Just be *nice!*

What the *Hulk?!*

Did you see how *strong* she is?

Wow. Thanks, Mol.

Man... that made me... *sleepy...*

Come on, time to move.

Wait, my mom's in the bottom of that *pool!*

She's gonna *drown!*

Your mom's a *murderer,* Karolina.
She's my *mom!*

All right. I'll fish her out.
I'm coming with you, Nico.
The rest of you get to the van and have the motor running. If we're not out in three minutes... leave *without* us.

So your mom's staff just... came out from *inside* of you?
Yeah, right after Gert's dad *cut* me.
I don't know how to describe it. It's almost like my... my *soul* puked it up. Thing seems to work *me* more than I work *it*.

I'm just glad you're alive.
I know this probably isn't the right time to talk about it, but when we... when we *kissed*, it was like this little island of *all right* in an ocean of horrible--
I agree, Alex.

This *isn't* the right time.

Here we go.

You think she's still alive?
I'm not doing mouth-to-mouth if she's not.

Uhn!
Oh, my God.
Check it out...

Remember how Mr. Yorkes said that Karolina's parents had some kind of *decoder ring,* the one that supposedly deciphers their Playbook of Evil?
What if *this* is the ring he was--

VERMIN!

You think you've *beaten* us? We haven't even used a *fraction* of our strength against you.
Once the kid gloves come off, your parents will *annihilate* you. We brought you children into this world...

...and *we* can take you out.

KRAK!

*Nice.*
Speak softly, etc., etc.

Alex, what I said before, I didn't mean--
No, you were right, Nico.
We have more *important* things to worry about...

Downtown Los Angeles
8:42 A.M.

Damn, Mrs. Dean's ring only seems to be decoding *every other word* of this Abstract thing. I just hope there's enough dirt in here to put our parents away for good.

You sure you know the way to the police station, Karolina?

Yeah, I got arrested a few years ago when my parents took me to a *peace rally.*

I still can't believe that was all just an *act.* And I can't believe I *fell* for it.
Don't be so hard on yourself, gorgeous. Didn't your mom and dad both win *Emmys?* It's like, lying about who they really are is what your parents are *best* at.

What are we *doing?* I have to go to *school!*
It's okay, Molly. We're just going on a little field trip.

But my... my parents didn't sign a *permission slip.*
And they're never going to sign one again, Mol. The sooner you accept that, the sooner you'll--
DEET-DA-DEET-DEET

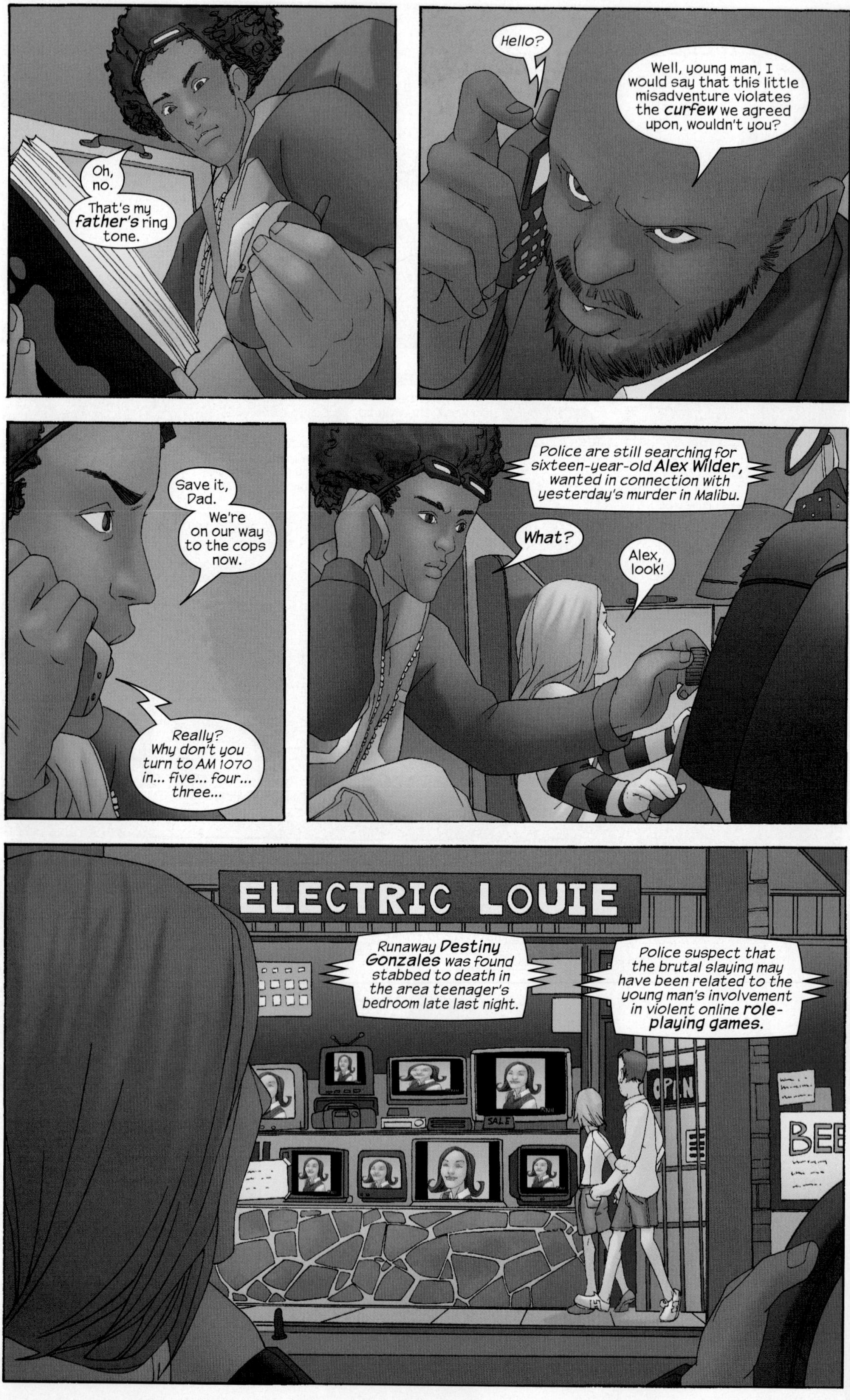

Oh, no.
That's my *father's* ring tone.

Hello?
Well, young man, I would say that this little misadventure violates the *curfew* we agreed upon, wouldn't you?

Save it, Dad.
We're on our way to the cops now.
Really? Why don't you turn to AM 1070 in... five... four... three...

Police are still searching for sixteen-year-old **Alex Wilder,** wanted in connection with yesterday's murder in Malibu.
**What?**
Alex, look!

ELECTRIC LOUIE
Runaway **Destiny Gonzales** was found stabbed to death in the area teenager's bedroom late last night.
Police suspect that the brutal slaying may have been related to the young man's involvement in violent online **role-playing games.**
SALE

That's the girl **you** killed!
Quiet, son. You'll miss the best part.

Authorities are reportedly also looking for other local teens who may have **helped** commit this crime.
SUNNY
In addition, the Amber Alert system has been activated for eleven-year-old Molly Hayes, who was allegedly **kidnapped** by this gang just a few hours ago.

Nice try, Dad. But we'll **prove** that you framed us.
Prove? To **whom**? The **police**? Who do you think tipped us off that you had run away in the first place? The **media**? Who do you think I ordered to release this story?

BREAK
NECK.
ELEVATE

Alex, my boy, this entire ***city*** belongs to The Pride.

But that doesn't mean we're despots. We're just concerned citizens who've made great sacrifices to make the world a better place for you.
And if you come home now, I swear that your mother and I will make all of your problems disappear.
I'd rather blow my own brains out than go back to your lies.

Listen to me, you little son of a--
Son of a what, Dad?
What exactly am I the son of?

Alex, honey, it's your mother. Don't do this. Please. The Pride... these men and women, they will hunt you down and gut you like a--
klick

Well, that didn't sound too good.
We're dead. Our parents, they... they control everything. We're fugitives from the entire world.
Then there's only one thing left to do.
What's that?

Fall off the face of the earth.

The Hayes Residence
9:01 A.M.
Molly, they... they have *Molly...*

We know, love.
But don't fear, Mr. and Mrs. Wilder have already put the back-up plan into effect.
The Minoru girl actually *struck* me.

Big deal, she froze *me* like a... a mystical *popsicle.*
How could they all *betray* us like this?

I'm not so sure that *all* of them have.

What is *that* supposed to mean?
When I was toweling off in your foyer, I noticed *this* on the floor.
It's a note.
*And?* What does it say?
"Mom and Dad-- I love you, and I know you have reasons for doing what you did. Don't worry, I'll always be loyal to you."
Good Lord, who wrote it?
Don't know. Thing's unsigned.
Well, well, well, The Pride suddenly has its very own ***mole.***
But who the hell is it?

Bronson Canyon
Griffith Park
10:27 A.M.
Are you nuts, Chase?
DANGER
GAMMA TESTING SITE LETHAL LEVELS OF RADIATION
The "amazing hiding spot" you've been bragging about is a cave?
Holy stupid ideas, Batman.
Actually, isn't this where they shot exteriors for the old Batman TV show?
Nah, that cave is closer to Franklin. This one's way off the beaten path. Nobody comes back here.
No wonder! Look at this sign!
DANGER
GAMMA TESTING SITE LETHAL LEVELS OF RADIATION!
Oh, I bought that off eBay. I put it up right after I found this place, just to make sure nobody tried to squat in my haunt.
This is awesome, Chase!
Hang on, kid. We're not even to the best part yet.
Crawl through here...

Where are we? I can't see anything!

Hey, whose hand was that?

Karolina, take off your inhibitor bracelet!

Oh, right!

Boys and girls, welcome to a little place I like to call... *The Hostel!*

Well, hostile is the right word for it. Looks like it was designed by M.C. Escher on crank.
Yeah, a few years ago, I read about a "missing mansion" in this weird book I stole from my old man... before he had a chance to read it himself, thankfully.
I guess some crazy actor built this joint up there back in the 1920s. From the looks of it, it got swallowed up during an earthquake and fell down here.
It doesn't seem very... stable.
RRRRRR
Easy, Old Lace.
Old Lace?
Yeah, that's her new name... to go with my new one.
From now on, I'd like to be called Arsenic.
What kind of lame codename is Arsenic and Old Lace?
First of all, watch a movie made before 1985.
Secondly, it's not a codename. I just don't want to be called Gertrude anymore.
That's the name they gave me.

That's a great idea, Ger... er, Arsenic.
From here on out, you can call me, um... Lucy in the Sky.
Well, my AIM handle is Sister Grimm.
I guess that works.
And my new name is... Neo.
You can't be Neo, Chase.
Why not?
Because you have to pick something original!
And what's so original about naming yourself after some ancient song?
Chase's name should be Talkback.
Hee.
Laugh it up... Bruiser.
Bruiser?
But I wanted to be Princess Powerful...

How about you, Alex?
Wilder.
My name is Alex Wilder.
I know, but--
I recognize that my parents have ruined that name, but I don't want to run from it.
I want to redeem it.
How?
By using all of these powers and weapons and... and resources to bring our parents to justice for everything they've done.
Alex, that could take years!
Fine. Until then, we can start to atone for our parents' crimes by helping people. We'll protect the world they're trying to destroy.
But at least half of us are wanted criminals now!
Yeah, John Walsh is probably already gunning for us.
Well, we can't just sit in here and wait to die. We'll have to wear disguises or something when we go out.
What are you talking about? Dressing up in costumes and... and playing super hero?
No offense, Alex, but isn't that sort of childish?
What's the alternative, "Arsenic"? Being an adult?
If that means turning into the people who raised us...

...I hope I *die* before I get old.
NEXT: TEENAGE WASTELAND

THIS LETTER APPEARED IN *RUNAWAYS #18*, FOLLOWED BY BRIAN K. VAUGHAN'S RESPONSE:

Team Runaways,

Last issue? What do you mean, LAST ISSUE? What the hell does that mean? Did you type it wrong? Were you thinking of something else, like maybe the *Sub-Marine*r or the *Smurfs*? How can there be a last issue when the story is obviously going to continue for years? You're some kind of wrong person. Have it looked into.

Your fan,
Joss Whedon

Yep, that's the real Joss Whedon, of *BUFFY*, *ASTONISHING X-MEN* and, uh, *ROSEANNE* fame. Cool, huh? But thanks to the vocal support of loyal readers like you (and Joss), I am thrilled to announce that this is NOT the last issue of *Runaways*. Our kids are going on a well-deserved vacation for a few short months, but the entire creative team will be bringing them back in early 2005 for *RUNAWAYS #1*! One chapter in the lives of our young heroes has ended, but an all-new, all-different one is about to begin.

I ♥ Wolverine
Hey Guys!
Just a quick note, wanted to tell every-one how good it's been working with all of you, & how much I look for-ward to the 2nd season.
This Team OWNS.
♥ you all!
xoxoxo
Christina

THANK YOU NOTE FROM CHRISTINA STRAIN

RUNAWAYS

# EXPANDED PROPOSAL BY BRIAN K. VAUGHAN

At some point in their lives, all young people believe that their parents are the most evil people alive.

But what if they really are?

When six young friends discover that their parents are actually super-villains, the teenagers agree to run away from their respective homes. Using the unique gifts they inherited (or stole) from their immoral mothers and fathers, these fugitive heroes vow to do everything they can to atone for their parents' crimes.

Smallville meets Harry Potter in this all-ages action/adventure series.

THE PREMISE

Alex Wilder always knew that there was something strange about his parents, a happily married couple of wealthy Los Angeles socialites. Instead of family reunions, the Wilders host annual get-togethers with five other families. While the adults discuss their charity program in private, Alex has to hang out with their kids, an oddball collection of five other only children.

At one of these gatherings, the six teenagers make a horrifying discovery. They learn that their parents actually lead something called The Pride, an underworld organization of criminal kingpins, mad scientists, alien warlords, mutant terrorists, tyrannical time-travelers, and dark wizards. Working largely in secret to obtain complete world dominion, these all-new villains make Dr. Doom look like Dr. Evil.

The kids try to tell the authorities what they've learned, but the police are either disbelieving or under the far-reaching influence of the Pride. With no one else to turn to, the six teens agree to run away from their homes, but not before they pilfer strange technology and mystical devices from their corrupt parents.

Now on the run from their enraged families (some of whom want the children killed), the Runaways take up residence in the Hostel, an underground youth hotel buried during a California earthquake. In this unique, totally accessible new corner of the Marvel Universe, the would-be heroes give themselves new names, new attire, and a new purpose... to protect the community, right the wrongs of their parents, and one day bring the Pride to justice.

Still, the fruit usually doesn't fall too far from the tree, and some Runaways will have to fight the temptation to follow in their parents' footsteps. Matters will grow even more complicated when it becomes apparent that one of the Runaways may actually be a mole, loyal to the lethal Pride.

THE CHARACTERS

Wilder - The oldest of the Runaways, Alex Wilder is a seventeen-year-old African-American male. Though he has no powers, Wilder is a brilliant young strategist with a passion for directors like Hitchcock and online games like EverQuest. Now co-leader of the Runaways, Wilder is ashamed that his role-model parents are actually two criminal kingpins who fund the Pride's terrorist activities, and he intends to do whatever it takes to bring them down.

Sister Grimm - Rachel Messina is the sixteen-year-old daughter of two of the world's oldest and most powerful dark magicians (who now pose as wealthy antique dealers). Before she runs away from home, the crafty raven-haired girl grabs a dusty tome filled with spells. Now calling herself "Sister Grimm," Rachel struggles to master these black magicks (despite her religious background). The other co-leader of the Runaways, Sister Grimm is romantically attached to Wilder.

Lucy in the Sky - Leslie Dean is a stunningly beautiful, happy-go-lucky, sixteen-year-old girl who never imagined that her parents were actually alien warlords (who hide from intergalactic police under the guise of earthly real estate magnates). In some ways, Leslie has it much harder than her fellow Runaways. Not only does she discover the awful truth about her parents, but she also learns that she's really an alien. Still, this revelation becomes a lot easier to accept when she finds that her otherworldly physiology allows her to fly. Taking her codename from a favorite song, "Lucy in the Sky" will discover new and wonderful powers every day she's on the team. If only she could get ________ to fall in love with her, her life would be complete.

Talkback - The team's only other male (tradition be damned!), John Stein is the sixteen-year-old son of two "mad scientists," a couple that claims to be nothing more than successful software engineers. Inheriting little of his parents' technical know-how (he would rather play lacrosse), John is nevertheless able to obtain experimental hi-tech gauntlets before escaping from his broken home. Dubbed "Talkback" by his teammates, John hates taking orders, preferring to fly headlong into battle. Thankfully, his extensive array of hi-tech gadgets usually prevents him from getting hurt. Talkback is more than a bit obsessed with Leslie, and he's constantly vying for her attention.

Arsenic & Old Lace - Ferociously independent (if a little socially inept), Gertie Yorkes isn't the least bit surprised to hear that her retired parents are actually time-traveling despots from an apocalyptic future. Eager to leave home, she takes something from her parents hidden sub-basement before jetting, a ferocious velociraptor genetically engineered in the 87th Century to telepathically serve its master (in this case, Gertie). Calling herself "Arsenic," Gertie names her loyal dinosaur "Old Lace." Together, they're an extremely formidable, extremely odd duo.

Bruiser - The youngest member of the Runaways, Molly Hayes is the thirteen-year-old homo superior daughter of two Hollywood actors (who are actually mutant terrorists). Shortly before joining the team, Molly discovers that her genetic makeup grants her extraordinary strength. The little girl can bench a city bus without breaking a sweat... but she'd much rather watch the new Kylie Minogue video on TRL. Gertie (who acts like an overprotective older sister around Molly), jokingly nicknames her "Bruiser," a handle that seems preposterous given her sweet and innocent exterior. Molly claims that she's eager to do the right thing, but deep down, she just misses her Mommy and Daddy.

THE TONE

I started getting into comics when I was about twelve, but I had almost no interest in books like Power Pack or Teen Titans. Even though they were well crafted, they seemed like they were aimed at little kids (which no twelve-year-olds think of themselves as). I was more interested in books like X-Men, cool stories about badass outcasts (which is what most twelve-year-olds think of themselves as).

Now that Grant Morrison is writing X-Men for readers my age, Marvel could use a new all-ages series that's smart and edgy, but also PG-rated and absolutely continuity-free. I'm confident The Runaways can be that book.

Combining action, romance, humor, and some Harry Potter-style darkness, The Runaways is a series that older readers will definitely enjoy, and a book that retailers can confidently put into the hands of younger customers (if such a thing still exists).

THE STORIES

Like the excellent first arc of Ultimate Spider-Man, we'll be starting from square one and taking time to tell a character-driven origin story. These are my tentative plans for our first six issues:

Issue #1 - We open with Spider-Man and Daredevil working together to capture the Hulk... only to reveal that this is actually teenager Alex Wilder playing an online role-playing game starring his favorite real-world superheroes. (This will quickly establish that our protagonist is a young, intelligent, contemporary aspiring hero.) Alex's parents barge in and order him off the computer. Their guests are about to arrive.

The Wilders are soon joined by five other wealthy families, each made up of two loving parents and their single child. As the grown-ups discuss their charity work in private, Alex is forced to entertain the other kids (which is almost as awkward as having to hang out with those strange second cousins you only see at Thanksgiving). Here, we quickly establish the basic relationships of the six teenagers: Alex and goth Rachel are attracted to each other, flighty Leslie has a secret crush on ________, jock John has a secret crush on Leslie, and everyone hates misfit Gertie, except for prepubescent Molly, who trusts the older girl enough to ask her about the "strange things" happening to her body.

Instead of playing Playstation like they normally do, the six teens decide to spy on their parents' private meeting. Watching from a secret passage Alex recently discovered, the kids are amazed to see the way the adults behave behind closed doors. But when Alex's father produces an orphaned infant (obtained on the black market) from inside a box, the suddenly troubled kids tell young Molly to shut her eyes. The teens watch in horror as their parents reveal their unique powers, and use them to perform some kind of dark sacrificial ritual.

After the baby is killed (off-panel!), the adults smile and toast, "To the end of the world as we know it." From their hidden vantage point behind a one-way mirror, the kids react with fear and disbelief. Suddenly, one of the adults turns to the mirror, and asks, "What was that noise?"

Issue #2 - The adults burst into the secret passageway... only to find it empty. They make sure that their children are still playing Playstation in another room, and return to their vile work. Alone again, the kids drop their calm facades and freak out. Did they really see what they thought they saw, or was it some kind of game? What the hell are they supposed to do now?

Rather than confront their apparently evil elders and possibly end up dead, the kids resolve to meet up in secret later that night (except for young Molly, who they decide to keep in the dark about this). They struggle to act natural when their parents finally exit their "meeting," and exchange terse farewells before leaving.

Escaping their homes after midnight, the kids reconvene at the parking lot of a nearby mall (minus young Molly). After much deliberation, they decide to call the Avengers and tell them about their parents' secret lives as super-villains. But when the Avengers' hotline is busy, they're forced to call a homicide detective at a local precinct. When the man laughs at their "evil parents" story, the kids realize that they're going to have to find some hard evidence before anyone will believe them. Alex found nothing when he searched his home for the infant's corpse or any of the murder weapons used in the ritual, so the group decides to pile in John's van and check out Gertie's house next.

Sneaking inside (Gertie's parents are asleep), the kids soon find a secret passageway much like the one in Alex's house. Spelunking down a deep corridor, they suddenly hear something behind them. The kids turn to see a giant velociraptor baring its fangs!

Issue #3 - The group screams in terror, but the dinosaur politely bows in front of Gertie. A note around its neck explains that this beast was meant to be a gift for Gertie in the event of her time-traveling parents' death. The cyborg raptor responds only to her commands, and is trained to protect her from the countless enemies Gertie's evil mother and father have apparently made over the years. The kids scour the rest of the catacombs for evidence, but retreat after finding nothing (dinosaur in tow).

As relationships and jealousy blossom, the kids head to Rachel's home, where they eventually find a passageway in the woods behind her house. Inside, they discover the book of spells Rachel's warlock parents used during the sacrifice. But because of her Christian faith, Rachel refuses to try any of the "black spells" found inside. Desperate for more damning evidence, the group decides to press on.

Finally, the kids try the secret chamber inside Leslie's house (her parents are out of town), where the attractive young woman finds out about her alien heritage. At first, she's completely horrified, but when Leslie discovers that the "medical bracelet" she's been forced to wear her whole life is the only thing inhibiting her from using her power of flight, she perks right up. Unfortunately, the group finds nothing else of value, and so moves on to John's home.

Meanwhile, back at the police precinct the kids phoned last issue, the Captain asks one of his detectives about the strange call that came in earlier. The Captain laughs nervously when he hears the story about the kids and their "super-villain parents," but he soon retreats to his office and calls Alex's father, whispering, "My Lord, I think we may have a problem..."

Issue #4 - Inside a secret lab underneath John's house, the young athlete is shocked to learn that his parents appear to be brilliant mad scientists. How could a guy who flunked biology be the son of two scientific geniuses, the other kids wonder. John tries on a pair of hi-tech gauntlets, when he suddenly hears a voice say, "That's enough, children. I just received a troubling call from Alex's father. Your little scavenger hunt is over." The kids turn around to see John's parents, both wielding huge sci-fi weapons!

Gertie's pet raptor leaps to her defense, but is quickly neutralized. Alex leads the others in a decent fight, but they're no match for the two more experienced adults. The teenagers are almost defeated, when Rachel sacrifices her beliefs to cast a black spell that temporarily overpowers John's parents.

The kids are able to retreat, but Alex soon gets a call on his cell phone. It's his mother, who says, "Alex, you need to stop this immediately... or I'm afraid we'll have no choice but to do something terrible to your young friend Molly."

Issue #5 - Sick at the thought of anything happening to Molly, our heroes foolishly decide to rescue their youngest companion from the home of her evil mutant parents.

Naturally, when they arrive, the group is greeted by several adults, Rachel's mother, Gertie's father, and both of Molly's parents (who are using their perplexed daughter as a human shield). The teenagers use

what little they've learned about their weapons/abilities, but they're once again soundly defeated by their more powerful elders.

Molly's father is about to hurt her friend Gertie, when Molly suddenly breaks free of her mother's grasp and punches her father through a wall! Clearly, when Molly was telling Gertie about the changes happening to her body back in Issue #1, she didn't mean puberty... she meant the onset of her mutant powers!

This briefly turns the tide of the fight, and the kids barely escape alive. Before fleeing the house with Molly, Alex grabs something called "The Compendium," an encrypted book that appears to have information about the adults' clandestine organization, "The Pride."

Though they never found the body of the slain infant, the teenagers decide that they now have more than enough information to take to the authorities. But when one of the kids turns on the radio in John's van, they hear a startling report. The police are looking for a teenager named Alex Wilder... who apparently killed an infant in his own home. When interviewed, Alex's parents say that this murder "might have something to do with their son's involvement in violent online role-playing games," and the cops suspect that some of Alex's friends may have helped commit this heinous act.

Simultaneously, the framed kids say, "Oh, $#@*."

Issue #6 - Realizing that even the police are under the control of their parents' evil empire, our heroes are now wanted fugitives with no one to turn to. Rachel reveals that she has a secret hiding place that she's been going to since she was a little girl, and the group is forced to take shelter in this abandoned underground youth hospice.

Frightened and overwhelmed, the six formerly wealthy kids now have nothing but each other. Betrayed by their duplicitous families, the teenagers are united by their desire to do whatever it takes to destroy the Pride, and to right their parents' wrongs. Creating codenames and disguises for themselves, an unlikely new team of heroes is born.

Finally, in an intriguing epilogue to our first arc, we revisit the teenagers' assembled parents. The Pride is distraught by the evening's turn of events, but heartened by an unsigned electronic communiqué they receive. It reads, "Mom and Dad - I love you, and I know you have reasons for doing what you did. Don't worry, I will always be loyal to you."

The Next Arc - As the Runaways start to decode the Compendium they stole in our last storyline, they begin to realize just how powerful their parents really are, and how much damage their secret organization has done over the last twenty years. Accepting that they're not yet ready to take on the Pride, the masked teenagers decide to use their newfound powers to protect the community (and maybe atone for some of their parents' sins in the process). They start by attempting to capture a group of bank robbers terrorizing Los Angeles... but the Runaways soon discover that being a superhero isn't as easy as it looks on TV.

Meanwhile, romances and feuds between team members continue to develop. And elsewhere, the Pride comes up with an ambitious plan to lure their "wayward" children back home.